Interspersed

Tayra Barnes

BookLeaf
Publishing

India | USA | UK

Presentation by *BookLeaf Publishing*

Web: www.bookleafpub.com

E-mail: info@bookleafpub.com

ISBN: 978-93-5744-341-8

First edition 2022

DEDICATION

To Talia, my very first fan. I couldn't have done it without you.

To Tequinya, for her hands of god and heart of gold.

ACKNOWLEDGEMENT

Writing is a journey I've long been on, alone at first; never again.

Special thanks to, my sisters, Talia Barnes, Sammi Barnes and Shari Barnes. My brother, Taran Barnes. My Dad, Christopher Barnes. My best friend, Cameron Duncan. The Cosmo to my Wanda, Ben Mitchell. Tequinya Valentine, for letting me use her incredible art on the cover. And lastly Stephen Henderson, an English teacher like no other.

PREFACE

Growing up, reading always brought me the most joy. There was nothing better than escaping into the pages of a high fantasy or murder mystery. My passion for reading is what inspired me to be a writer. I want to give others the joy that reading gives me. In this debut collection I hope to inspire you, the reader and maybe (just maybe) give you some joy too.

Cruel Mistress

Devil in disguise, luminescent eyes
Such a pretty face, did she make you cry?

Jester in the sheets, Queen upon her throne
Hide behind a smile, pick apart the bones

A weary heart left broken, blood upon the floor
Hear the children in the street, the knock upon
the door

A slip into abyss
I'm lifting off the ground
I hope they understand why I no longer am
around

Wishing Well

Your heart is like a wishing well
I tossed a coin and watched as it fell

I cried into your depths, hoping I could fill you
Gave you love and hope, rather than dust and
mildew

You took my wishes gladly, held them in your
abyss
But your heart it was still empty, cold just like
your kiss

Now you have a piece of me, and I'll wish again
no more
But at night I can still hear you, begging at my
door

I hope that you will leave soon, as I'm weeping
on the floor
Pray it was a bad dream and wish again some
more

The Map of Me

3

I am but a faint line in a map full of scars
Blink and you'd miss me
Don't tear me apart

Powdered and polished, overlooked from the
start
Stretch me and pull me
You'll see me, I'm stark

Hiding in plain sight, a mark on your wrist
You struggle once more
Oh, look I'm a twin

Calliope; Inspired by Lord of The Rings

Down the pastures rolling, beyond the soaring
hills
Across the roads of old and tumbling water rills
Through many a cave and forest
Across mountaintop and cliff
The battle finally won, their hearts began to lift
They crossed the golden sands and turned
towards the sun
The journey long was over, to home they'd
surely run

Far and wide a cry was heard, of joyous pure
delight
They climbed aboard Queen Calliope and sailed
into the night

Talia

I came into the world, when she was very young
Whenever there was trouble, to help she'd surely
run

I had a lot of anger, from the day that I was
sprung
Fought so many people but she was number one

Years went by and then my eyes were opened to
the truth
No matter my resistance
I'll always need you

You helped with my ups and downs
Saw me through to the very end

So here's my way of saying thanks
To Talia, my best friend

Strangers

Sometimes I lie awake at night and wonder
where you are
The wound of you I carry now; the memory but
a scar
So many words to choose from
None now left to say
I threw away my chance, when I watched you
walk away
A fleeting glimpse is all I get
Like a match struck in the dark

The life I knew has faded
Now strangers, we depart

The Ballad of Us

I found a heart of gold and mined for all its
worth
Opal eyes left empty; the way summer leaves a
hearth

Porcelain skin is crumbling, breaking beneath
my fingers
Peeling back your layers, a burning pain that
lingers

Broken down and dusty, carried by the wind
Turn the ash to flowers and wait for you in
spring

Come here, come here dear sweetheart
I know you walk again
I knew it when I heard the birds rejoice and start
to sing

Branches broke and twisted
Leaves are drenched in blood
Caught off guard, surprised I am
Who knew you'd try to run?

You should be scared my lovely, if you try to
flee again
I'll hunt you like a fox and darling you're the hen

She-Devil

Down the darkened halls; from whence the
royals came
There walked a fair young lady
A king's forgotten dame
Hiding in the shadows
A throne ravaged by sin
An innocent heart grew wicked, waiting in the
wings

She donned a mask and played her part
Like a puppet on a string
She'll hold you like an angel

But the Devil plays to win

Growing Pains

The girl I used be
Has gone and said goodbye
I don't know why she left me
But for Her I'll always try

What does it truly mean?
To forget just who you are
Some days are outright easy
Others are awfully hard

I struggle with my image
Who I am, I still don't know
But they say that life's a journey
Lets see how far I go

Mind Inmate

I've fallen down a rabbit hole
My mind a slippery slope
Drowning in my neurons
Will my depression float?

If I found a ladder I'd take out the rope
And use it to drag the air from my throat

I'm stranded at sea without a boat
Can I outlive myself?

Nobody knows

The Final Rest

12

The fields, they wait with bated breath
A sob the only sound
A heart left empty heaves with grief
Like a hole within the ground

Goodbyes feel like fire
That burn a grieving throat
Where I've gone, you'll have to wait
Before you too will know

Tuck me in and say farewell
Leave a kiss upon my brow
Close the lid and seal my fate
The final rest is now

Me, Myself and I

My patchwork heart
A mosaic of rainbow pieces
Like a pane of stained church glass

My curious mind
A collection of faces and places and things
Tokens of time more precious than rings

My wandering soul
Surrounded by love
Searches for more in the stars up above

Cosmo

Will you be my Sunny Bank?
In the midst of rocky shores

Will you find a way to reach me?
When I hide behind my walls

Through all the trips and tumbles
For all my faults and flaws

Could you find a way to love me
Would you let my heart touch yours?

Flight of The Dancers

A quiet day at midnight
As wind rolls off the hills
A peep or shout could not be heard from
churches to sawmills

A town of ghosts and memories lost stays cold
until the morning
Frost begins to melt away when the sun begins a
dawning

Water runs like tears of sorrow across old
pebbled streets
And run it did, away from here, to rivers fast and
deep
Fleeing now, homeward bound
From the town that always sleeps

When springtime comes, you'll hear not mum,
but birds upon the sill
A song of old, centuries lost; few words and
many trills

A tale is told of long ago, a town of merry music
Of a new found world, the wanderers spoke,
before leaving to pursue it

Whispers ran like wildfire, across every nook
and hill
And spark it did, the hearts of many; a
long-forgotten thrill

Racing across the fields of old, towards the
setting sun
They heard within, the call of Hope; their
journey had begun

Minds alight with fancied flight and promised
gold from newfound lands
The dancers rode into the night and came not
once again

Hidden Sin: Inspired by The Dark Artifices

Broken souls led twisted ways
And left the world in disarray
A head once proud, now bowed in shame
A man once whole, never the same

A friendly face, the perfect disguise
A driving madness behind the eyes
A tongue of silver; pretty lies
Killer with the charming smile

Revenge, oh how it tastes so sweet
Like deadly sins sat down to feast

Sleight of hand; a magician show
Now your so called friends all know
So my dear it's time to go
To reap the seeds that you have sowed

Amendment now it's best to show
May God have mercy on your soul

Spiral

Pages of a diary
Left blank for several years
Hopes and dreams-of-waking
Fell short of listening ears

Torn up thoughts lie careless
Like weeds upon the earth
Growing across my psyche
Are the thorns of my self-worth

Lost in my reflection
With no one staring back
Trapped inside a spiral; there's just no turning
back

The old house down the street

Every day I walk by
The old house down the street
If you cared to visit; not a living soul you'd meet
But sometimes when it's quiet
And the timing is just right
I can see the curtains moving
From the corner of my eye
Still the house lies empty

In the morning I ride past
Racing down the path
And glimpse the shrouded faces, standing at the
glass
I swerve aside in fear and tumble from the seat
My bike is swept away, by the car it flew
beneath
I gaze up at the house, checking wall to wall
But when I look into the windows; there's no
one there at all
Every day I walk by

Late one afternoon
I stop outside the gate
Curiosity beckons; home can surely wait

I skip along the pavers and climb the groaning
porch
When my friends begin to call me
Before I've reached the door
Still the house lies empty

The visions start at midnight
A vibrant world's within
Hidden behind the walls
Of a house that's crumbling
I wake up with the sun and watch it fill the sky
As soon as I am dressed
Every day I walk by

I knocked upon the wood
And heard no sound within
But when I tried the handle; it opened with a
spring
I stepped across the threshold and followed the
dancing lights
That night I had a tour; of many wondrous sights
Now the door, is shut once more
Locked to you and me
And though it's filled with secrets
Still the house lies empty

In my youth, I learned the truth
About the old house down the street
I know I'll never go back
But it's a secret that I keep
Cross my heart and hope to die
Every day I walk by
Still the house lies empty

The Sun or Us

22

Where the daisies dance and meet
And wave to the sun under my feet

A bed of warmth and perfume sweet
Embraced by gold and summer heat

Days beneath a sunset veil
Orange, purple, pink and blue
Fall short at the sight of you

And Darling if I had to choose
The Sun or us
I'd bid Her adieu

Hunger

23

Yours is the flesh of sustenance
Eyes a bountiful stream
Cherry blossom lips
Sweet like maple leaves

Knelt at the feet Lucifer
I'd surely need to be; your lustre but a vision
Fore I'd tire of your feast

I Wonder

I wonder where you are
Are you bundled up at home
Or driving in your car
Do you miss me too? Please

Do you think of where I am
On days of hours long
Does it hurt you like it hurts me
When I listen to our song
I wonder where you are

When we parted ways I never thought
That life could get much worse
But this distance now between us
Feels more like a curse
Do you miss me too? Please

I was at a standstill
Life was racing past
I met a few new people
And still we are apart
I wonder where you are

I used to think it funny, other times were sad
Am I going crazy?

Is it really all that bad?
Lately I've been angry
But that just isn't right
This battle we've been caught in
Isn't ours to fight
Do you miss me too? Please

Although it's never easy
Often times I'm glad
I know that you are happy
For that, I can't be mad
But still I have to know
To put my mind at ease
I wonder where you are
Do you miss me too? Please

Recovery

I lost a piece of me, when I said goodbye to you
Four long years of waiting
Change was nothing new
A brand-new house, a brand-new school
People come and go
But when asked if you would come again, the
only word was "no"

I've been forgotten in many ways
Throughout 18 years of life
But I'd never guess, the way you left
Without me by your side

Now you've gone and found a place
Where I can't ruin your life
But joke's on you, Mother dear
I'm better off without you in mine

I broke out of my shell
Became someone I didn't like
Walked a path that many tread
Unknown to my young feet
And met myself alone one night
When I should've been asleep

And so began
A brand-new chapter
In a story titled "Me"
Of a bright young woman's journey
That led to recovery.

9 789357 443418